High-Interest READING

by
Laurie Gilbert

Cover Design by
Matthew Van Zomeren

Inside Illustrations by
Don O'Connor

Publisher
Instructional Fair • TS Denison
Grand Rapids, Michigan 49544

Permission to Reproduce

About the Author

Laurie Gilbert received her M.A. degree from Utah State University and her B.A. degree in elementary education from Wheaton College. Laurie has a richly varied background, including homeschooling her children and teaching in bilingual classrooms. She spent a year teaching in Honduras, and she continues to tutor Spanish-speaking students in the U.S. Laurie's volunteer experiences as a girls' club coordinator for 10 years contributes to her understanding of children and how they learn.

Credits

Author: Laurie Gilbert
Cover Design: Matthew Van Zomeren
Inside Illustrations: Don O'Connor
Project Director/Editor: Sharon Kirkwood
Editors: Lisa Hancock, Eunice Kuiper
Typesetting/Layout: Pat Geasler

Standard Book Number: 1-56822-612-8
High-Interest Reading
Copyright © 1998 by Instructional Fair • TS Denison
2400 Turner NW
Grand Rapids, Michigan 49544

Table of Contents

A Starry-Eyed Coyote

Have you ever looked up at the night sky and wondered how all the stars got there? People from nations and tribes all over the world have developed myths to explain them. Here is a myth from the Hopi of the Southwest United States.

Before the people came, there were only animals on Earth. The animals all worked together to make the rest of the world, except for lazy Coyote who refused to do any work. While the others built the mountains, Coyote only laughed at their hard work. When they brought the rivers and made them flow across the land, Coyote came and lapped up the water. When the other animals made the trees, Coyote found a shady spot and fell asleep so he missed the rest of their creation. The animals dug valleys between the mountains, and holes for the rivers to fill lakes. They made flowers of all colors to decorate the hillsides. Last of all they made thousands of round, shiny objects to complete the world. Some of the animals wanted to hang them from trees. Some thought they should be sprinkled across the desert while others wanted to put them on mountaintops where they would best catch the light of the sun. By nightfall they couldn't agree, so they left them in a pile and went to bed. Coyote woke up from his nap and saw the pile. He sniffed at them and then picked one up. It wasn't good to eat, so he threw it into the air. He looked at another and decided it wasn't good for anything either, so he threw it into the air also. One by one Coyote sniffed and looked at each one and threw them into the air. When they were all gone, he looked up at the sky and saw little spots of light scattered throughout the darkness. This is how the stars came to be.

What was the main idea of this story?

_____

_____

_____

_____

_____

How did the mountains, rivers, and trees come to be?

_____

_____

_____

_____

What did Coyote do while the other animals worked?

_____

_____

_____

_____

What were some ideas for using the shiny objects?

_____

_____

_____

_____

How did the stars come to be in the sky?

_____

_____

_____

I'm So Bored!

Do you know that three of America's favorite pastimes came about as a result of someone being bored?

James Naismith was a physical education teacher in the 1890s when he invented the game of basketball. During the months of warm weather he was able to have his students play football outside, but when the weather became too cold and snowy, they had to go into the gym. The students were bored with exercises and wanted an exciting game instead. Naismith hung a peach basket off the balcony on each end of the gym and had 2 teams of 9 players each dribble or pass a soccer ball down the court until they could shoot it into the basket. It was an instant success. The game of basketball had been invented, and now, 100 years later, it is one of the most popular sports in the country.

Another pastime started when students at Yale University ordered pies from the Frisbie Pie Company. When they finished the pies and their studies, they were bored and looking for something to do. One student discovered that with a flick of the wrist, the pie plate would glide through the air. Soon frisbie-ing, or pie-tin catch became a popular game on campus. In 1948, Walter Morrison made the game safer by making plastic discs in the shape of flying saucers. But the brand name Frisbee, which originated from the bakery name, stuck. Today you can find Frisbees in every park and on every playground.

J.L. Plimpton loved to ice skate. So when winter would come to an end, he was always bored. But in 1863, he designed a skate with wheels that could travel on land. Now he was able to enjoy an activity in the warm months similar to his favorite winter pastime. It worked so well that he decided to share his idea with others. He built a large skating rink in Rhode Island where people could try his roller skates. Roller skates have been improved over the years, and are now joined by their cousins, in-line skates, as popular sporting equipment.

Mapping is one way of organizing or outlining information. Fill in the map below with details from the story. There is a blank space at the bottom for you. Draw a picture of what you might invent; then fill in the other information about it.

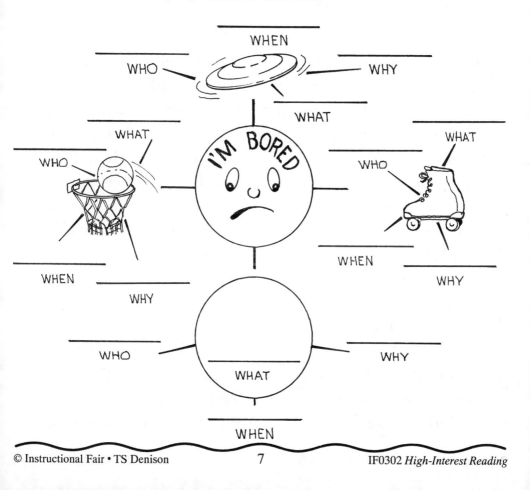

Little Red Riding Hood and the Confused Wolf

Story #1

One day Little Red Riding Hood's mother fixed a basket of treats for Little Red's grandmother who lived on the other side of the woods.

"Take this basket to your grandmother. Do not talk to any strangers or stray from the path because the wolf might harm you."

Little Red Riding Hood agreed and started off through the woods. Just a short way off the path were some beautiful wild flowers. Little Red thought how much her grandmother would enjoy them. So she left the path to pick them. She hadn't gone very far when she ran into a wolf who asked where she was going. When he found out about Grandmother, he ran ahead, locked Grandma in the closet and was waiting in the bed when Little Red arrived.

"What big teeth you have, Grandma!" exclaimed Little Red.

"The better to eat you!" growled the wolf as he leaped out of bed. Just at that moment, Grandma knocked down the door, hitting the wolf on the head.

Story #2

"Beware of people," warned Little Wolf's mother as he ran out of the den to play. He had not gone far before he saw a little girl. He watched from behind a tree and thought, "She's so small and she doesn't look like she'd hurt anyone." So he walked up to her and asked what she was doing. Little Wolf took the girl's response as an invitation to play. Since he had 4 legs and she had only 2, he beat her to Grandma's house. When Grandma saw him, she screamed and ran into the closet. Little Wolf jumped into the bed to surprise the girl. He was licking his lips thinking about the delicious cakes she was carrying when she walked into the house.

"What big teeth you have, Grandma!" exclaimed the girl.

Little Wolf was laughing so hard, thinking he had fooled her, that he could hardly choke out, "The better to eat your cakes!"

Little Red never heard the end of the sentence because she was screaming so loudly.

Just then something hit Little Wolf on the head.

You just read two versions of the same story, each from a different point of view. Story #_____ was told from a wolf's point of view, while story #_____ was told from a human's point of view. Fill in the chart below telling how each story explains the incident.

Incidents	Story #1	Story #2
Mother's warning at the beginning		
The meeting in the woods of Little Red & Little Wolf		
How Grandma ended up in the closet and why the wolf climbed in the bed		
The ending of the story		

Wolfways

Wolves are often pictured in fairy tales as ferocious animals, always ready to attack and kill anything they can catch. But are wolves really that vicious? Let's find out.

Wolves are very social animals and live together in packs of anywhere from two or three to twenty wolves. Each pack has a male leader and a female leader called the alpha wolves. The members of a pack generally cooperate and get along well with one another.

Wolves are often pictured howling at the moon. Scientists have discovered that the howl is actually a way of locating other wolves, assembling the pack, sounding an alarm, or announcing a kill. Besides their howl, wolves use body language to communicate. The position of their back, neck, ears, and tail send distinct messages that other wolves understand.

Because they are hunters, wolves have a strong sense of smell, much greater than a human's sense of smell. That means not only can they smell their prey while it's still far away, but they also know where their enemies are. They usually feed on large animals such as deer and elk, with the pack working together to bring down their prey. They kill only when they are hungry and need to eat.

Who are the worst enemies of wolves? Humans! Wolves are more likely to run from you than to attack. Wolves were once common across much of North America, but are now rare and can be found only in remote wooded regions.

The following sentences are either facts that are true, or opinions stating how someone might feel about something. Write **F** beside a statement if it is a fact, or **O** if it is an opinion.

_____ 1. Wolves are big, bad, and ferocious.

_____ 2. Wolves live in packs.

_____ 3. I'd like to find a wolf in my yard.

_____ 4. A wolf pack is very large.

_____ 5. Members of wolf packs usually cooperate with one another.

_____ 6. Wolves like to howl at the moon.

_____ 7. A wolf's howl communicates a message to other wolves.

_____ 8. Wolves have a strong sense of smell.

_____ 9. Wolves hunt large animals.

_____ 10. Elk tastes better to a wolf than other animals.

_____ 11. When a wolf has its tail down, it is communicating a message to other wolves.

_____ 12. Wolves are scary animals.

Extension:

Here are some good books that will help you to find out more about wolves. *Julie of the Wolves* by Jean Craighead George, or *Snow Dog* by Jim Kjielgaard.

Score!

Justin dashed down the soccer field toward the goal. "I'm open!" he shouted. "Pass the ball."

Brian kicked the ball toward Justin, but before he could reach it, one of the opponents darted in and booted the ball away.

"Don't worry. We'll get it next time," yelled the coach as Brian sprinted back to regain possession of the ball. This time he dribbled out the wing beating opponent after opponent. He centered the ball, and Justin bolted up just in time to kick it toward the goal. It was caught by the goalie. "Nice try, you almost had it!" shouted the coach as the team rushed back down the field.

The opponents now had possession of the ball. They flew past the first defender, took a shot at the goal and missed.

"Make this one count!" bellowed the goalie as he kicked the ball out to his team. "Time is almost out."

Brian was determined to score. He raced down the field. He could hear the fans in the background. "Go! Score!" they roared.

In a last effort the whole team charged down to help him out. They passed the ball around the opponents, and worked closer and closer to the goal. The shot was good!

"Congratulations! You guys were great! What a game! What a team!" cheered the fans.

Synonyms are different words with similar meanings. In the story, there are several different words used in place of *ran* and *screamed*. See if you can find them and list them below.

Ran

_____

_____

_____

_____

_____

_____

_____

Screamed

_____

_____

_____

_____

_____

Write two or three synonyms for each of these words:

great   **small**   **said**

_____   _____   _____

_____   _____   _____

_____   _____   _____

Extension:

A thesaurus is a book that lists synonyms. Use a thesaurus and see if you can add to your lists above. Why do you think it is important to know synonyms for words? _____

_____

The Best Batch

Is there anything better than coming home from school and sitting down to a snack of milk and chocolate-chip cookies? Here is a great recipe. Be sure to get permission before you bake them.

Chewy Chocolate-Chip Cookies

Preheat oven to 375°.

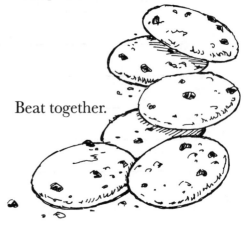

1 cup butter
1 cup white sugar
1 cup brown sugar   } Beat together.
1 teaspoon vanilla
2 eggs

2 cups of flour
2 1/2 cups of oatmeal
1/2 teaspoon salt   } Mix together and gradually
1 teaspoon baking powder   add to butter mixture.
1 teaspoon baking soda

Stir in 12 ounces of chocolate chips (you may also add 1 cup of chopped nuts and/or 1 cup of raisins if desired).

Roll into golf-ball size balls and place 2 inches apart on an ungreased cookie sheet. Bake at 375° for approximately 6-8 minutes for chewy cookies. Bake longer for crispier cookies. Remove from pan. Cool. Eat and enjoy. Makes 4 to 5 dozen cookies.

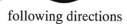

Complete the following.

1. List the ingredients you need for this cookie recipe.

    _____

    _____

    _____

2. Number these directions in the correct order.

    _____ Measure and mix flour, oatmeal, salt, baking powder, and soda.

    _____ Bake for 6-8 minutes.

    _____ Get permission to bake.

    _____ Roll into golf-ball size balls.

    _____ Cool.

    _____ Measure and mix butter, sugars, eggs, and vanilla.

    _____ Preheat oven.

    _____ Place 2 inches apart on an ungreased cookie sheet.

    _____ Eat and enjoy.

    _____ Gradually add flour mixture to butter mixture.

    _____ Remove from pan.

    _____ Add chocolate chips (and nuts and raisins if desired).

3. How many cookies does this recipe make? _____

4. What might happen if you didn't follow the directions?

    _____

A Perfect Day at Camp

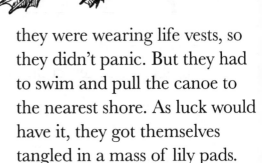

It was a perfect day at Camp Wake-Em-Up. Shannon and Krista were planning to spend their free time sailing on the lake. Unfortunately, their cabin was the farthest from the lake, and by the time they got there all the sailboats had been checked out.

Fortunately, there was still a rowboat left. However, when they took it out, it began to sink because it had a leak. Since they were only 5 feet from shore, the waterfront director was able to rescue them quickly. But the boat was useless for their afternoon adventure. By the time they got back on shore, a canoe had been returned, so they got in and began paddling across the lake. When they were three-fourths of the way, they dropped a paddle. When Shannon leaned over the side to grab it, you guessed it. The canoe tipped over! Of course they were wearing life vests, so they didn't panic. But they had to swim and pull the canoe to the nearest shore. As luck would have it, they got themselves tangled in a mass of lily pads.

Sitting on one of the lily pads was a welcome surprise: a big bullfrog that was sure to win the frog-jumping contest at the evening activity. But when Krista reached out for him, he jumped away, landing in the canoe. Because it took Shannon and Krista much longer to get back to camp, they missed dinner. But they were on time for the contest. However, Bullfrog didn't want to jump. Just then a fly buzzed by. When Bullfrog jumped to catch it, he won the contest.

It turned out to be a perfect day at camp.

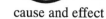

Fill in the chart below. A cause is what makes something happen. An effect is what happens as a result.

Cause	Effect
The cabin was a long way from the lake.	
	They used a rowboat.
	They used a canoe.
Shannon reached for the paddle.	
They were wearing life vests.	
	They found a frog.
Krista reached for the frog.	
	They were late for dinner.
A fly buzzed by.	

"I Have a Dream"

Martin Luther King, Jr. was a great civil rights leader in the United States. One day he gave a famous speech. In it he said, "I have a dream!" Here are some of the things he dreamed about: That one day all the people in the United States really would be equal; that his children would not be judged by their skin color, but by their character. He dreamed that the sons of former slaves and the sons of former slave owners could sit down and talk together as brothers. He dreamed that black boys and girls and white boys and girls could all hold hands and walk together. He dreamed that all men could be brothers and work together, pray together, struggle to- gether, and be free together. He wanted freedom to ring from every village, and every city in every state of the coun- try. He dreamed that all the

people in our country, no matter what the color of their skin or what beliefs they had or how old or young they were, would live in peace with each other.

Martin Luther King wasn't able to see that dream fulfilled during his lifetime. But every January, we set aside a special holiday in his memory to celebrate the ideas of his dream.

1. Circle the statement that best summarizes Martin Luther King's dream.

   a. All children would have the same skin color.

   b. Everyone in this country would live in peace.

   c. Slave owners would set slaves free.

2. Circle the reason why we have a special holiday in January.

   a. To remember Martin Luther King and his belief in co-operation between the races and equal rights for all

   b. To have a day off from school

   c. To celebrate people's dreams

3. Cross out the things that were not a part of King's dream.

All people are equal.

There will be no old people.

Peace!

All men would work, pray, and struggle together.

The U.S. would be better than other countries.

Sons of slaves and sons of slave owners would talk together as brothers.

Skin color doesn't matter.

Freedom everywhere.

There would be a holiday to celebrate equal rights.

Pecos Bill

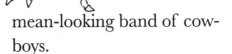

Pecos Bill was the toughest cowboy who ever lived. When he was only a baby, his family decided to move west. On the way he bounced out of the wagon. No one even noticed until they were too far away to do anything about it. Fortunately for Bill, a coyote found him and brought him home and raised him. It wasn't until he was 17, when he met a cowboy, that Bill realized he wasn't a coyote.

"What do you mean I'm no coyote? I got fleas and I howl at the moon."

"We all do that. You don't have a tail," responded the cowboy. That convinced Bill. As he started off across the plain, a mountain lion attacked him. Bill wrestled with him until the lion gave up. He decided to keep the mountain lion for his horse. He jumped on the lion's back and rode off. Before long he ran into a mean-looking band of cowboys.

"Who's boss here?" asked Bill.

"I was, but you are now," responded the meanest one of all.

"Well, what are you doing with all these cows?" Bill inquired.

"Nothing," they replied. "There's too many of them."

"Folks in Kansas need cows. Let's run them up there. It will give us something to do." And so the cattle drive was invented.

On another occasion, a cyclone blew in. Everyone ran away scared except Bill. He jumped on the cyclone and rode it without a saddle as if it were a bucking bronco.

"Yeehaw!" Bill yelled as he was carried across several states. When the cyclone wouldn't calm down, he got angry at it and squeezed it so hard, it cried. Its tears fell and formed the Grand Canyon.

A tall tale is a story about a person whose characteristics are much bigger than real life. There are many versions of this tale. In the box below are several character traits. Circle only the traits that describe Pecos Bill. Then circle them in the Wordsearch.

big	timid	brave	crazy	strong
gentle	tough	friendly	clean	loud
leader	independent	quiet	shy	mean
wild	sweet	pretty	inventive	bad manners

O	Y	L	D	N	E	I	**R**	F	B	R	G	T	I	A
P	N	Q	U	B	R	E	P	D	S	P	**A**	C	E	D
C	H	**T**	O	R	J	U	M	R	E	M	R	O	L	L
I	G	R	L	A	W	E	E	V	S	A	N	**T**	E	U
P	N	F	S	V	P	N	I	G	Z	E	K	N	A	**L**
J	O	I	H	**E**	N	T	F	Y	D	L	I	W	D	H
W	R	G	R	A	N	Q	L	T	**S**	U	C	V	E	T
N	T	S	M	E	E	T	Y	L	O	D	M	F	R	O
A	S	D	V	O	G	I	B	S	P	U	E	**A**	T	B
H	A	N	D	Y	N	R	**K**	A	X	L	G	B	V	I
B	I	N	D	E	P	**E**	N	D	E	N	T	H	Z	F

Pick out the bold print letters. Write them in order from top to bottom as they appear in the Wordsearch to find out what Pecos Bill used for a lasso. _____

Secret Messages

Are you tired of having your pesky little sister read your diary? Maybe you have a top-secret message you need to pass on to a friend. Using a secret code could be your solution.

People all through history have used secret codes to keep unwanted readers from understanding their messages.

Can you read this?

Leonardo da Vinci, an Italian artist and inventor, used mirror writing for all his notes. The notes were written backward so that you would have to hold them in front of a mirror to read them.

L fdph, L vdz, L frqtxhuhg.

The code above is a quotation from Julius Caesar, a Roman emperor who developed his secret code by shifting the letters of the alphabet to match another letter. It may have looked like this:

a b c d e f g h i j k l m n o p q r s t u v w x y z

d e f g h i j k l m n o p q r s t u v w x y z a b c

The intended letter on the top row matches the code letter on the bottom. The letter *a* would be written as *d* in the code. The word *cat* would be written *fdw*.

Mary Stuart, Queen of Scotland, used a secret code when planning to kill her cousin, Queen Elizabeth of England. However, her code was discovered and broken. It was Mary Stuart who ended up being executed instead.

George Washington used invisible ink during the Revolutionary War to send secret messages about battles. He wrote the messages

with lemon juice which couldn't be seen until they were held up to a light.

Benjamin Franklin liked to use picture codes, or rebuses, just for fun. Here's an example:

monk + key = monkey

There are many ways to use secret codes to be sure that your messages are read by only certain eyes.

Hold the first secret message in the story up to a mirror and write the message on the line.

_____

Try writing your name in mirror writing.

_____

Use Julius Caesar's code to decipher his message on the previous page:

_____

Use that same code to write your name:

_____

Try decoding these rebuses.

-L + I + 2 + = E + Z + - DY + EZ + - AT =

Write a rebus message of your own.

As Good As New

It's as black as ink out here in the pasture, and I'm as tired as an old shoe. But even if I were in my bed, I don't think I'd be sleeping like a baby tonight.

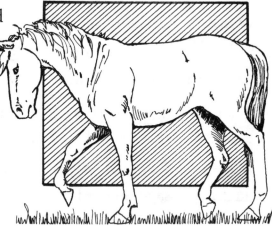

Last summer for my birthday, my parents gave me my dream horse. Her name is Goldie. She is a beautiful Palomino, and her coat sparkles like gold when the sun shines on it. Every day I brush her until she feels as smooth as silk. I love to watch her gallop around the pasture. She runs like the wind and looks so carefree with her mane and tail flowing behind her. I hope I'll see her run that way again.

Yesterday, after I fed her, I forgot to close the door to the feed shed. She got into the grain and ate like a pig, which is very unhealthy for a horse. The veterinarian said I have to watch her like a hawk tonight to be sure she doesn't colic. That's a very bad stomachache. Because he also said I should keep her moving, I have walked her around and around the pasture until I feel like we're on a merry-go-round.

Now the sun is finally beginning to peek over the horizon, and Goldie seems as content as a kitten. I think she's going to be as good as new. That makes me feel as happy as a dog with a fresh bone.

A simile is a comparison using the word *as*. The title of the story, "As Good As New," is an example. You can also use the word *like*: She ran like the wind.

1. Underline the 12 similes in the story.

2. Write the similes that help to describe the horse.

   _____

   _____

3. What simile lets you know that the horse ate a lot from the feed shed?

   _____

4. Sometimes we use well-known similes to describe traits. Fill in the blanks with a word that is usually associated with each animal. Write one of your own for the last one.

   a) as _____ as a mouse

   b) as _____ as a fox

   c) as _____ as a snail

   d) as _____ as a puppy

   e) as _____ as a _____

5. There can be many similes to describe the same thing. In this story, how did the author describe her happy feeling?

   _____

   What are some other similes you might use to describe a happy feeling? _____

   _____

Sadako

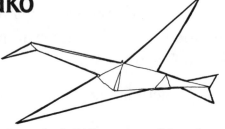

Sadako Sasaki sat on her hospital bed folding an origami paper crane. There is a Japanese legend that says the crane lives for 1,000 years. If a sick person folds 1,000 paper cranes, the gods will make him/her well.

On August 6, 1945, when Sadako was a baby, her city was hit by a nuclear bomb. Many people were killed, including Sadako's grandmother.

Sadako was growing up to be a responsible girl and a talented runner. In fact, she was the fastest on her sixth-grade relay team. One day Sadako started feeling dizzy and collapsed after running. Her parents took her to the doctor and discovered she had leukemia, a disease that had come as a result of the bomb. The disease had been living in her body for ten years.

She was admitted to the hospital. Whenever friends came to visit, they helped Sadako fold her paper cranes and soon they were hanging from strings all around her room. Before 1,000 cranes were folded, Sadako fell asleep and never woke up again.

The children of Japan built a statue in honor of Sadako and all the other victims of the atomic bomb. Every year children all around the world fold paper cranes and send them to the mayor of the city of Hiroshima. They are then placed at the statue to celebrate peace day on August 6. On the statue, which is an image of Sadako with her hands raised to the sky holding a golden crane, are these words: "This is our cry. This is our prayer. Peace in the world."

Events in Sadako's life can be divided into 3 categories: before her illness, during her illness, and after her illness. In each column write 3 events which happened during each time period.

Before	During	After

Extension: Read more about Sadako in *Sadako and the Thousand Paper Cranes* by Eleanor Coerr.

Take a Closer Look

Imagine you have just been out running through a field playing fetch with your dog. You come back home hungry and thirsty, but just as you walk into the house your mom takes one look and sends you and the dog back outside to pick off all the burrs. After a half hour at the task, you become annoyed, wishing there were no such thing as a burr. But what if you took a closer look?

That's exactly what Georges de Mestral, a Swiss engineer, did in 1941, when he and his dog came home covered with burrs from a walk. Instead of just pulling them off and throwing them aside, he took one and decided to look at it under a microscope. He was curious to understand what made it cling to everything. He discovered that it was made of tiny barbed hooks that stuck to the loops of thread in his clothing. It reminded him of fasteners such as zippers, hooks and eyes, and buttons, and he had an idea. For 17 years he experimented with his idea until he developed the perfect fastener—a group of tiny barbed hooks that can stick to little loops of thread—Velcro. Not only can it be used to fasten shoes closed, but it is strong enough to fasten astronauts to the floor of their spaceship!

Georges de Mestral was making an analogy when he compared the burr on his clothing to a fastener. An analogy is a way of comparing two different things and finding something similar. He compared the way a burr sticks two things together with the way a clothing fastener binds cloth together.

Below is a list of items in nature. Use your creative and critical thinking skills to decide to what you might compare each item.

spider web _____

dandelion flower seed _____

maple tree seed _____

beehive _____

swallow's nest _____

clam shell _____

prairie dog town _____

Choose one of the analogies above or one of your own ideas to create a useful invention. Draw and describe it below.

_____

_____

_____

_____

_____

_____

The Trail Ride

The horses leave the corral as usual, calmly walking nose to tail along the trail they know so well. They could probably do it with their eyes closed. I sit back and relax because my horse will just plod along behind the others. I gaze out across the hay fields and rolling hills to the Grand Tetons towering in the distance. I wonder what it was like to be a cowboy a hundred years ago.

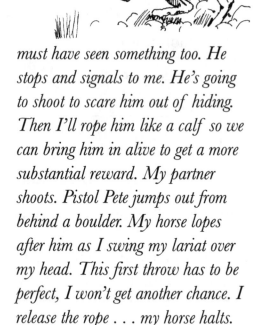

Suddenly, I am galloping through the sagebrush toward the Tetons where the famous outlaw Pistol Pete is thought to be hiding. As we reach the bottom of the mountain, our posse decides to split up and travel in pairs up different trails. Our pace slows as we carefully wind around rocks and trees, knowing Pistol Pete could be hiding behind any of them. As we come near to the ridge, I notice a slight movement. It could be Pete. Either way I'd have to approach with caution. My partner must have seen something too. He stops and signals to me. He's going to shoot to scare him out of hiding. Then I'll rope him like a calf so we can bring him in alive to get a more substantial reward. My partner shoots. Pistol Pete jumps out from behind a boulder. My horse lopes after him as I swing my lariat over my head. This first throw has to be perfect, I won't get another chance. I release the rope . . . my horse halts.

We're back at the corral already. "Ride's over. Dismount and tie your horse to the fence. We hope you enjoyed your ride and will come ride with us again at the Rockin' W Ranch."

An antonym is a word having a meaning opposite to another word. On the blank, write an antonym from the Word Bank to replace the word in italics in each sentence.

Word Bank				
ran	walking	unknown	boldly	huge
leave	excitedly	small	grasped	mount

1. The horses *plodded* along the familiar trail. _____

2. The *famous* outlaw hid behind the boulder. _____

3. We watched the riders *approach*. _____

4. I *released* the lariat. _____

5. There was a *slight* movement on the ridge. _____

6. The horses were *galloping* across the prairie. _____

7. It's time to *dismount*. _____

8. We crept *carefully* around the bushes. _____

9. There was a *substantial* reward for capturing the outlaw.

   _____

10. The horses *calmly* followed one another out of the corral.

   _____

Ridiculous Rabbits and Red Radishes

Rabbits really relish red radishes. So when Farmer Robinson ran to the railroad to ride away for the rest of the day, Roberta and Rebecca Rabbit raced to the radish patch on his ranch. They ripped the radishes from the ground and ravenously devoured them raw, row by row, then reclined under a rosebush and relaxed. When Farmer Robinson returned, he remarked in a rage, "What rascal raided my ranch and reaped my ripe radishes?" The rabbits revived when they heard him roar and realized they had better remove themselves right away. They rose from their resting place and rapidly ran down the road. Before Farmer Robinson had time to react, they had reached the ridge and were out of range.

Farmer Robinson recovered from his rage. He rambled to his storage shed and retrieved his rusty rake and rapidly replanted the radishes. He rigged up a ridiculous scarecrow from some old rags and raised it up on a rail. He then relaxed in his rocking chair to read the paper. Suddenly he heard such a racket outside, he thought the rabbits must have returned. He reached for his rifle to rid himself of the rascals. He was radiant as he dreamed of roasted rabbit ribs for his repast (dinner). Rather than finding the rabbits, he found ravens in the raspberry bushes.

In the morning when Farmer Robinson went outside, he discovered his radishes were again ruined. He refused to give up and replanted the garden. This time he remem-

bered that red hot peppers are revolting to rabbits, so he planted a red pepper in place of each radish. When Roberta and Rebecca Rabbit returned to the ranch to replenish their supply of radishes, they realized they had been tricked by Farmer Robinson and never returned again.

Alliteration is the use of words which repeat the same beginning sound. Tongue twisters are good examples.

1. Write one sentence from the story that illustrates

    alliteration. _____

    _____

2. Write a sentence using as many of the words below as possible. (You may add different endings to the words.)

book	brought	Beth	brush	bop
Billy	bicycle	bat	baboon	bang
Bob	big	boat	boot	bag

    _____

    _____

3. Make a list of 10 words that start with the same letter. Include nouns, verbs, and adjectives.

    _____   _____   _____

    _____   _____   _____

    _____   _____   _____

    Now write a sentence using several of those words.

Flagging Down the Flags

All countries of the world fly flags using colors and symbols to represent their countries. Our own United States flag has thirteen red and white stripes to represent the 13 original colonies and 50 white stars on a blue field to represent the 50 states. Here are interesting facts about other flags.

Canada: The Canadian flag uses a red maple leaf set on a field of white with a red stripe on each side. The leaf has been a symbol of Canada since the nineteenth century.

Austria: The legend of the Austrian flag says that it is red like the bloodstained robe of Duke Leopold V. The only part of his robe that stayed white was the area under his wide belt, so there is a wide white stripe across the middle of the flag.

Scandinavia (Norway, Sweden, Denmark, Finland): All the flags of the Scandinavian countries show a cross, which according to a legend, was the symbol on a flag that fell from heaven in a battle between the Danish and the Estonians in 1219. The Danish flag is red with a white cross; Sweden's is blue with a yellow cross; Finland's is white with a blue cross; Norway's is red with a blue cross outlined in white.

Japan: The Japanese flag is white to represent purity and integrity. The red sun in the center represents sincerity, brightness, and warmth.

Using some of the descriptions in the article, color the flags below.

Canada

Austria

Sweden

Denmark

Finland

Japan

Design a flag that represents you or your school. Write a description of it.

_____

_____

_____

Design a flag and have a friend color it according to your description.

_____

_____

_____

Ben's Journal

Feb. 9, 1997

Tomorrow is the big day. I've studied so hard for the past three weeks, I think I could spell these words in my sleep. But what if I get nervous and mess up? What if someone else knows more words than I know? Rebecca always wins when we practice at school. I just want to do the best that I can. Mom has helped me every night after supper. She says that studying and learning are more important, in the long run, than winning.

Feb. 10, 1997

I did it! Well, I didn't win first place, but I came in second, and I'm really proud of that. At first I was scared when I looked out and saw all those people in the audience. I was afraid I'd forget everything. But then I told myself, "You studied hard. You know all those words. Come on, you can do it!" My first word was *indicate*: i-n-d-i-c-a-t-e. It was easy. Then I knew I could do the rest of them, too. The only word that really stumped me was *cannibal*. I spelled it c-a-n-n-i-b-l-e—oops. Rebecca spelled it right, along with her last word: *hydraulics*. Oh well, I won a dictionary and had my picture taken for the newspaper. When I came home, my family had a party to celebrate! Tomorrow, I start studying for next year's contest.

Answer Key

High-Interest Reading—Grade 4

Page 5

What was the main idea of this story?

How the stars got in the sky

How did the mountains, rivers, and trees come to be?

The animals made them.

What did Coyote do while the other animals worked?

He laughed and slept.

What were some ideas for using the shiny objects?

*Hang on trees
Put on mountaintops
Sprinkle across desert*

How did the stars come to be in the sky?

The coyote threw them up there one by one.

Page 7

Mapping is one way of organizing or outlining information. Fill in the map below with details from the story. There is a blank space at the bottom for you. Draw a picture of what you might invent; then fill in the other information about it.

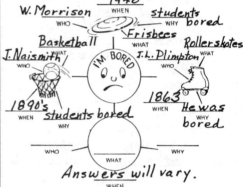

W. Morrison WHO — *1948* WHEN — *Frisbees* — *students* WHY *bored*

Basketball WHAT

J. Naismith WHO

1890's WHEN — *students bored* WHY

J. L. Plimpton WHO — *Rollerskates* WHAT

1863 WHEN — *He was bored* WHY

WHO — WHAT — WHY — WHEN

Answers will vary.

Page 9

Story #2 told from a wolf's point of view.
Story #1 told from a human's point of view.

Story #1

Don't stray from path; Beware of wolf.

Strayed off path; Wolf asked where she was going.

Wolf locked Grandma in the closet.

Wolf was knocked out. Grandma and Little Red ran to Red Riding Hood's house.

Story #2

Beware of people.

Wolf wanted to befriend Red Riding Hood, so he asked where she was going.

Grandma hid in the closet; Wolf hid in the bed.

Mother Wolf worried about her son.

Page 11

The following sentences are either facts that are true, or opinions stating how someone might feel about something. Write **F** beside a statement if it is a fact, or **O** if it is an opinion.

O 1. Wolves are big, bad, and ferocious.

F 2. Wolves live in packs.

O 3. I'd like to find a wolf in my yard.

O 4. A wolf pack is very large.

F 5. Members of wolf packs usually cooperate with one another.

O 6. Wolves like to howl at the moon.

F 7. A wolf's howl communicates a message to other wolves.

F 8. Wolves have a strong sense of smell.

F 9. Wolves hunt large animals.

O 10. Elk tastes better to a wolf than other animals.

E 11. When a wolf has its tail down, it is communicating a message to other wolves.

O 12. Wolves are scary animals.

Page 13

Synonyms are different words with similar meanings. In the story, there are several different words used in place of *ran* and *screamed*. See if you can find them and list them below.

Ran	Screamed
dashed	shouted
darted	yelled
sprinted	bellowed
bolted	roared
rushed	cheered
flew	
raced	
charged	

Write two or three synonyms for each of these words:

Suggestions:

great	small	said
excellent	little	replied
magnificent	tiny	responded

Extension: Answers will vary.

Page 15

1. List the ingredients you need for this cookie recipe.
   butter, white and brown sugar, vanilla, eggs, flour, oatmeal, salt, baking powder, baking soda

2. Number these directions in the correct order.

   4 Measure and mix flour, oatmeal, salt, baking powder, and soda.

   9 Bake for 6-8 minutes.

   1 Get permission to bake.

   7 Roll into golf-ball size balls.

   11 Cool.

   3 Measure and mix butter, sugars, eggs, and vanilla.

   2 Preheat oven.

   ___ Place 2 inches apart on an ungreased cookie sheet.

   12 Eat and enjoy.

   5 Gradually add flour mixture to butter mixture.

   10 Remove from pan.

   6 Add chocolate chips (and nuts and raisins if desired).

3. 4-5 dozen.
4. Answers will vary.

Page 17

Cause	Effect
The cabin was a long way from the lake.	No sailboats were left.
There were no sailboats, so...	They used a rowboat.
The rowboat sank	They used a canoe.
Shannon reached for the paddle.	The canoe tipped over.
They were wearing life vests.	They didn't drown.
They got stuck in lily pads	They found a frog.
Krista reached for the frog.	Frog jumped in the boat.
Had only 1 paddle	They were late for dinner.
A fly buzzed by.	Frog jumped to catch it.

Page 19

1. b. Everyone in this country would live in peace.
2. a. To remember Martin Luther King and his belief in cooperation between the races and equal rights for all

3. Cross out the things that were not a part of King's dream.

All people are equal.
There will be no old people.
Peace!
All men would work, pray, and struggle together.
The U.S. would be better than other countries.
Sons of slaves and sons of slave owners would talk together as brothers.
Skin color doesn't matter.
Freedom everywhere.
There would be a holiday to celebrate equal rights.

Page 21

A tall tale is a story about a person whose characteristics are much bigger than real life. There are many versions of this tale. In the box below are several character traits. Circle only the traits that describe Pecos Bill in the Wordsearch.

big	timid	brave	crazy	strong
gentle	tough	friendly	clean	loud
leader	independent	quiet	shy	mean
wild	sweet	pretty	inventive	bad manners

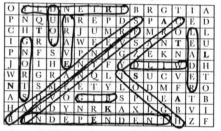

Pick out the bold print letters. Write them in order from top to bottom as they appear in the Wordsearch to find out what Pecos Bill used for a lasso. *Rattlesnake*

Page 23

monk + key = monkey

There are many ways to use secret codes to be sure that your messages are read by only certain eyes.

Hold the first secret message in the story up to a mirror and write the message on the line.

Can you read this?

Try writing your name in mirror writing.

___

Use Julius Caesar's code to decipher his message on the previous page:

I came, I saw, I conquered.

Use that same code to write your name:

___

Try decoding these rebuses.

See eye to eye.

Easy come, easy go!

Write a rebus message of your own. *Easy come, easy go!*

Page 24

It's as black as ink out here in the pasture, and I'm as tired as an old shoe. But even if I were in my bed, I don't think I'd be sleeping like a baby tonight.

Last summer for my birthday, my parents gave me my dream horse. Her name is Goldie. She is a beautiful Palomino, and her coat sparkles like gold when the sun shines on it. Every day I brush her until she feels as smooth as silk. I love to watch her gallop around the pasture. She runs like the wind and looks so carefree with her mane and tail flowing behind her. I hope I'll see her run that way again.

Yesterday, after I fed her, I forgot to close the door to the feed shed. She got into the grain and ate like a pig, which is very unhealthy for a horse. The veterinarian said I have to watch her like a hawk tonight to be sure she doesn't colic. That's a very bad stomach-ache. Because he also said I should keep her moving, I have walked her around and around the pasture until I feel like we're on a merry-go-round.

Now the sun is finally beginning to peek over the horizon, and Goldie seems as content as a kitten. I think she's going to be as good as new. That makes me feel as happy as a dog with a fresh bone.

Page 25

1. Underline the 12 similes in the story.

2. Write the similes that help to describe the horse. *sparkles like gold; runs like the wind; smooth as silk*

3. What simile lets you know that the horse ate a lot from the feed shed? *He ate like a pig.*

4. Sometimes we use well-known similes to describe traits. Fill in the blanks with a word that is usually associated with each animal. Write one of your own for the last one.
   a) as *tiny* as a mouse
   b) as *sly* as a fox
   c) as *slow* as a snail
   d) as *playful* as a puppy
   e) as ___ as a *Answers will vary.*

5. There can be many similes to describe the same thing. In this story, how did the author describe her happy feeling? *...like a dog with a fresh bone*
   What are some other similes you might use to describe a happy feeling? *Answers will vary.*

Page 27

The events of Sadako's life can be divided into 3 categories: before her illness, during her illness, and after her illness. In each column write 3 events which happened during each time period.

Before	During	After
1. city was hit by a bomb	1. Sadako folded paper cranes.	1. Children in Japan built peace monument
2. Sadako's grandmother was killed	2. Was dizzy and felt a lump on her neck	2. Children from around the world send paper cranes to Japan.
3. Many people were killed	3. Went to the doctor	3. Celebrate Peace Day, August 6.
4. Sadako grew to be a responsible person	4. Admitted to hospital	
5. She was a fast runner.	5. Friends visited and helped fold paper cranes.	

Page 29

Possible answers:

Below is a list of items in nature. Use your creative and critical thinking skills to decide to what you might compare each item.

spider web *lace, fly catcher*

dandelion flower seed *umbrella, parachute*

maple tree seed *helicopter, propeller*

beehive *hat, apartments*

swallow's nest *bowl, plant holder*

clam shell *fan, shallow dish*

prairie dog town *subway system*

Choose one of the analogies above or one of your own ideas to create a useful invention. Draw and describe it below.

Answers will vary.

Page 31

1. The horses *plodded* along the familiar trail. *ran*
2. The *famous* outlaw hid behind the boulder. *unknown*
3. We watched the riders *approach*. *leave*
4. I *released* the lariat. *grasped*
5. There was a *slight* movement on the ridge. *huge*
6. The horses were *galloping* across the prairie. *walking*
7. It's time to *dismount*. *mount*
8. We crept *carefully* around the bushes. *boldly*
9. There was a *substantial* reward for capturing the outlaw. *small*
10. The horses *calmly* followed one another out of the corral. *excitedly*

Page 33

1. Selections will vary.
2. Sentences will vary.
3. Answers will vary.

Page 35

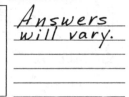

Canada   Austria   Sweden

Denmark   Finland   Japan

Design a flag that represents you or your school. Write a description of it.

Designs will vary.

Design a flag and have a friend color it according to your description.

Page 37

1. About what big event was Ben writing in his journal?

   Spelling Bee

2. Circle the words that best describe how Ben was feeling the day before the event.

   (confident)   (anxious)   tired   happy

3. Circle the phrase that best describes how Ben felt about winning second place.

   a) upset because he didn't win first place

   b) angry at the person who beat him

   c) (happy because he did his best)

4. How did Ben get over his fear of being in front of an audience? _He knew he was prepared._

5. Circle the phrase that you think describes how Ben prepared for the contest.

   Ben . . .

   a) just looked over the list once or twice.

   b) (studied very hard over a three-week period.)

   c) thought he could depend on being smart and didn't even look at the words.

Page 39

Number the steps for building a pyramid in the correct sequence.

_5_ Stones were rolled in on logs.

_1_ The site was chosen, cleared of sand and rubble, and the ground was leveled.

_4_ The causeway was built from the Nile River to the pyramid site, so stones could be dragged along it.

_10_ The stones were cleaned, and the ramps were removed.

_7_ The first layer of stones was laid.

_2_ The stones were cut at quarries.

_8_ Ramps were built so stones could be rolled up to the next level.

_6_ The passageway to the tomb and the tomb rooms were dug out.

_9_ The capstone was set in place.

_3_ The stones were shipped down the Nile River in boats.

Page 41

Diagrams will vary.

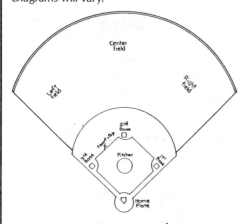

Record the score of the game at this point. _6_ Jets _6_ Birds

Pages 42 & 43

Creative Writing—all answers will vary.

Page 45

Unless you are a skateboarder, you probably found several new terms or vocabulary words. But the story provided contest clues.

Choose the correct answer by circling, filling in the blank, numbering, etc.

1. A skater is someone who: (a) rides a skateboard,) b) roller skates,   c) ice skates.

2. Number these tricks from easiest to most difficult:

   _2_ nose slide   _3_ kick flip   _1_ tick-tack

3. In which trick does the board spin around in the air? _Kick flip_

4. Describe an ollie. _Step back on tail like "popping a wheelie." Flick nose down with front foot so board is level under both feet._

Page 47

Complete each statement by circling the correct answer.

1. James Gurney's purpose in writing *Dinotopia* was . . .
   a. to explain how life once was on earth.
   b. (to show how humans and dinosaurs could live peacefully together.)
   c. to show how impossible it would be for humans and dinosaurs to live together.

2. One way dinosaurs helped people in *Dinotopia* was by . . .
   a. (providing transportation for people.)
   b. doing all the work.
   c. fighting all the enemies.

3. One way people helped the dinosaurs in the story was by . . .
   a. fighting the dinosaurs' enemies.
   b. painting pictures of them.
   c. (helping with the birth and raising of the young.)

4. The purpose of the article on *Dinotopia* was . . .
   a. to teach me about dinosaurs.
   b. (to interest me in reading the book for myself.)
   c. to answer the question of whether or not it is possible for dinosaurs and humans to live together peacefully.

Thinking Cap: Do you think a civilization like Dinotopia could be possible? Why or why not? _____
Answers will vary.

Page 48

"There is a problem at the zoo," explained Mr. Limb as the class (rode) down the (road) on the bus. All the animals are getting sick and no one can figure out why. Our class has been selected to help solve the mystery. When we arrive, each (pair) of students will be assigned to an animal. Take a (bear) with you for a snack. We'll meet back near the kitchen at 12:00 for lunch.

Ryan and Wes went to the lion's cage and found him lying on the ground, tied to a (stake.) While they watched, the zookeeper tossed him some food. He (ate) (eight) (steaks) and then lay down again.

Wade and Billy were assigned to the bear's cage. When they arrived, it looked (bare) because the (bear) was hiding in its cave.

Stacy and Lataya arrived at the (deer) enclosure just in time to see them feeding. "Oh

(dear)," exclaimed Stacy. That (doe) just ate a whole lump of (dough.) Now she's lying down in that hole."

As Nick and Latisha walked to the eagle's perch, Nick asked, "Is it legal to keep an ill eagle?"

To see the buffalo, Jill and Elise (flew) in a small (plane) over the (plains) at the edge of the zoo. "I wonder if buffalo catch a cold or (flu) like people do?" remarked Jill.

At the farm area of the zoo, Morgan said to Kristy, "Oh, (you) can tell that poor (ewe) isn't feeling well. What is it she's eating?"

As Tyler and Michael made their way to the elephant section, Tyler commented, "I (heard) that (herd) of elephants bellowing as we arrived. They sounded miserable!"

The fourth-grade class met

Page 49

Homophones are two or more words that sound the same but are spelled differently and have different meanings.

Read through the story again and circle the homophones. Connect each pair with a line. Example: We (rode) down the (road.)

Fill in the missing homophone for each of the following.

night: **knight**   some: **sum**   sun: **son**
two: **to, too**   which: **witch**   none: **nun**

Here are more sets of homophones. Write a sentence for each pair.

1. hare – hair: *Answers will vary.*

2. mane – main: _____

3. sail – sale: _____

4. male – mail: _____

Page 51

A   B   C

Write the letter of the resource you would use to . . .

A find a definition of a comet.
C find out current information about a comet.
B find out what a comet is made of.
C find out when you can see a specific comet in the sky.
B find out about the specific parts of a comet.
A find out the correct pronounciation of the word.

Answer the following.

1. What is a comet? *A heavenly body moving about the sun in an off-center orbit.*

2. Name the three parts of a comet. *head, coma, tail*

3. What is the name of the comet that was visible in March and April of 1997? *Hale-Bopp*

Page 53

When you write, you must use quotations marks whenever you are recording someone's words. Notice that quotation marks are placed around only whatever a person actually said.

Add quotation marks to the sentences below. Be sure to include any punctuation mark inside the quotation marks.

1. "What are you doing after school today?" asked Hannah.

2. "I don't know," replied Sarah. "Do you have any good ideas?"

3. Hannah responded, "I thought we could invite the new girl, Ashley, over and show her our doll collection."

Use quotation marks and write a short conversation between you and a friend.

Answers will vary.

Page 57

Under the picture write what each idiom really means.

Suggested answers:

You have nothing to say.   Someone is very happy.   Someone really special.

Drawings will vary.

Page 59

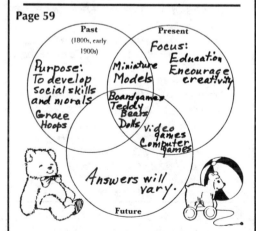

Past (1800s, early 1900s)

Purpose: To develop social skills and morals
Grace Hoops

Miniature Models
Board games
Teddy Bears
Dolls

Present

Focus: Education Encourage creativity

video games
Computer games

Answers will vary.

Future

Page 55

Match the letter of each of the numbers on the right to the corresponding word or phrase on the left.

E	years to build the *Titanic*	A. 1912
J	distance from Newfoundland	B. 850
M	people who died	C. 90
D	height of the *Titanic* (number of stories)	D. 10
		E. 3
B	length of the *Titanic*	F. hundreds of thousands
F	pounds of steel	
H	number of days on calm seas	G. 2,200
L	height of iceberg	H. 4
A	*Titanic* began maiden voyage	I. 5
N	time it took the *Titanic* to sink	J. 500
I	disaster struck on this day	K. 20.5
C	width of the *Titanic*	L. 60
K	speed the *Titanic* was traveling	M. 1,500
G	number of passengers on board	N. 2½

Page 61

Let's compare the lifestyles of these two girls, Kristy and Nicole. Fill in the chart below with specific examples from the story.

	Kristy	Nicole
Foods eaten during the day	grapefruit, egg, toast, milk, tuna sandwich, tacos, rice, apple, yogurt	Pop tart, bologna sandwich, chips, coke, chocolate pudding, hot dogs, french fries
Exercise	Rode bike to school, Soccer practice	None.
Care of body	Showered, Brushed teeth, To bed on time	Late to bed, Didn't brush teeth

We live in a throw-away society. When something is worn out, we throw it away and get something new. Some people think we can treat our bodies that way. But the body we have now is the only one we get so we must take proper care of it. Which of these girls will proabably have a healthier body? **Kristy**

Why? **She eats a well-balanced diet, exercises, & takes care of her body**

Tell why you think these best friends are drifting apart from one another.

Sugg. They have different habits and interests.

Page 63

Answer the following questions about Beverly Cleary.

1. Beverly Cleary has written more than 30 books for children. Based on the article, "Where Did Ramona Come From?" where did Cleary get her ideas for her stories?

   From her own childhood.

2. What are three qualities that make Beverly Cleary a good author?

   great imagination
   good observation skills
   creativity

3. What is one of Beverly Cleary's favorite pastimes?

   Reading books; going to the library

Thinking Cap: Think about your own life and the things that interest you. Make a list of experiences that you think could be turned into a series of fun and exciting short stories.

Extension: Read one of Beverly Cleary's books. *Henry Huggins* and *Ramona Quimby, Age 8,* are two of them.

Page 65

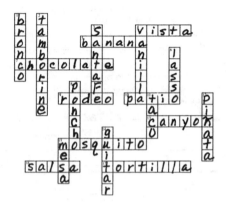

Page 67

This story is full of words whose sounds make you think of what they mean, such as "buzzing" and "fizzing." Use the clues to find words like these in the story. The letters in the boxes will spell the name of this type of word.

1. moving rapidly — *zooming*
2. sharp, metallic sound — *plink*
3. loud wailing cry — *howl*
4. deep sound like a cannon — *boom*
5. to bang noisily — *crashing*
6. soft, crackling sound — *rustling*
7. a short, quick sound — *popping*
8. a series of light, quick tapping sounds — *pitter-patter*
9. a long, thin cry — *whined*
10. a hissing noise — *sizzling*
11. a loud, smacking sound — *splat*

onomatopoeia

Page 69

Drawings will vary.

2. How did the grove of eucalyptus trees help the scientists to think of this plan?

   They saw how leaves collected drops of water from the fog.

3. What effect will this have on the village?

   They will now have water for drinking, cooking, batheing, & gardens.

4. What would be necessary in order for scientists to use this same idea to bring water to other desert areas?

   Fogs or clouds to pass over; large nets.

5. Will another area be too dry because of the way this water was taken for Chungungo? Why or why not? *No.*

   It was evaporating anyway when it went over the mountains.

Thinking Cap: Can you think of another way of bringing water to dry areas? *Answers will vary.*

Pages 70, 71, & 72

Creative Writing—answers will vary.

1. About what big event was Ben writing in his journal?

   _____

2. Circle the words that best describe how Ben was feeling the day before the event.

   confident   anxious   tired   happy

3. Circle the phrase that best describes how Ben felt about winning second place.

   a) upset because he didn't win first place

   b) angry at the person who beat him

   c) happy because he did his best

4. How did Ben get over his fear of being in front of an audience? _____

   _____

   _____

5. Circle the phrase that you think describes how Ben prepared for the contest.

   Ben . . .

   a) just looked over the list once or twice.

   b) studied very hard over a three-week period.

   c) thought he could depend on being smart and didn't even look at the words.

Thinking Cap: Write a journal entry about something you did or are going to do. Be sure to include your feelings about it.

Pyramids

Some of the largest buildings in the world are the great pyramids of Egypt that were built five thousand years ago. These were built as monuments to the kings and served as their tombs. The largest one stands as tall as a forty-story building. More than 2 million blocks of stone, each weighing $2^1/_2$ tons, were used to construct this pyramid. The builders did not have cranes or the other modern equipment that we have today. So how did they build them?

First a site was chosen, cleared of sand and rubble, and the ground leveled so the pyramid would sit evenly. Then the large stones were cut at quarries and shipped on boats down the Nile River. A long causeway, or stone road, was built from the river to the pyramid site, with a ramp for dragging the stones. The stones were rolled in on logs.

Before the actual building could begin, a passageway to the tomb room had to be dug underground. The tomb room was divided into several rooms. One of these rooms was the resting place for the king; others were storage rooms for all the king's possessions needed for the next life.

Once the tomb was completed, the first layer of stones was put in place. To get the stones to the next level, a ramp had to be constructed. Each time a level was completed, the ramp was raised and extended to reach to the next level. Some of the pyramids have more than 100 levels of stones. At the very top a capstone was set into place.

The workers then cleaned the stones so they would glisten in the sunlight. Lastly, they removed the ramps. A pyramid could take from 20 to 30 years to complete. They still stand today as magnificently as when they were built thousands of years ago.

Number the steps for building a pyramid in the correct sequence.

_____ Stones were rolled in on logs.

_____ The site was chosen, cleared of sand and rubble, and the ground was leveled.

_____ The causeway was built from the Nile River to the pyramid site, so stones could be dragged along it.

_____ The stones were cleaned, and the ramps were removed.

_____ The first layer of stones was laid.

_____ The stones were cut at quarries.

_____ Ramps were built so stones could be rolled up to the next level.

_____ The passageway to the tomb and the tomb rooms were dug out.

_____ The capstone was set in place.

_____ The stones were shipped down the Nile River in boats.

Take Me Out to the...

"Ladies and Gentlemen, this is the game that will decide the championship between the Jets and the Birds. It is the bottom of the ninth inning, with the Jets down by three runs. Do they have what it takes to win this game?

"The Jets' first batter, Sammy the Slugger, is at the plate, waiting for the first pitch. Low and outside, ball one. Here comes the second pitch. Slugger swings and connects. Ground ball to the shortstop, who bobbles it before throwing to first. Sammy is safe at first.

"The next batter, Striker, is at the plate. Foul ball, strike one. Another foul, strike two. On the third pitch, he swings and misses. Strike three! Out number one!

"Powerhitter Devon is now batting. He swings at the first pitch. It's a high fly to center. The centerfielder drops the ball. Devon is safe at first, but Sammy is tagged out at second!

"Lanky Leon walks up to the plate. He walks on four straight balls. Devon advances to second. Lefty is up next. He hits a grounder to right field, a double. The other runners each advance two bases.

"Harry the Hitter steps up to the plate. He watches two pitches go by before choosing *his* pitch. He hits a high ball over the left fielder's head. The runners on second and third score. Harry gets a triple.

"The next batter, Shorty, swings at the first pitch and misses. He connects with the next pitch. It's a short infield fly to the third baseman who easily catches it for the 3rd out. The inning is over, leaving Harry stranded at third base!"

Use the diagram of a baseball field to trace the route of each batter and figure out how many runs were scored. To make it easier, use a different colored pencil or crayon for each batter. With a dotted line of the same color, trace the path of each player's ball.

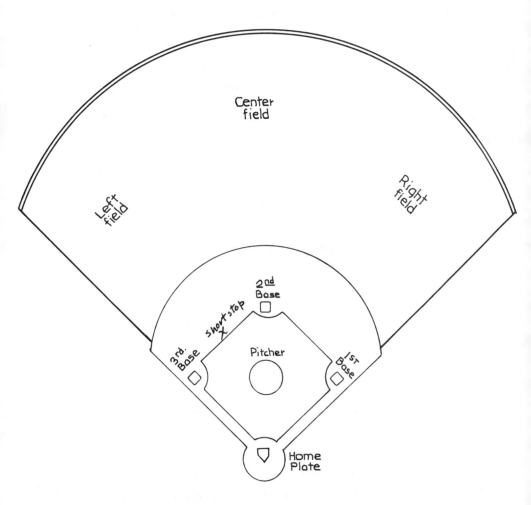

Record the score of the game at this point. _____ Jets __6__ Birds

---

Flight Fright!

Below is a mystery story that you will help write. Read the whole story first. Then go back and fill in the blanks. You will get to determine the guilty person and write the conclusion.

The ticket agent questioned me, "Have your bags been with you since you entered the airport? Has anyone you don't know asked you to carry something? Do you prefer a window or the aisle?"

Today is the day I've been waiting for since school got out. I get to fly all by myself to _____ to visit _____ . I just want to get on the plane and take off, but Mom started giving me last minute instructions. "Honey, _____ _____."

"I know, Mom. It's time to board. I'll see you in _____ ."

I buckle my seat belt to prepare for takeoff. I check the seat pocket in front of me: barf bag, magazine, emergency instructions, and an envelope printed in bold handwriting, "PLEASE DELIVER TO THE PILOT!" The pilot has just announced that we are heading down the runway for takeoff, so I have to wait until we're in the air.

As soon as the seat belt sign is turned off, I walk to the cockpit. "Excuse me, sir. I found this in the seat pocket."

The pilot takes the envelope, opens it, and reads out loud, "This plane is being hijacked to _____ . Be prepared to change routes. Cooperate, and no one will get hurt!"

The hijacker must be one of the passengers, but which one? I tell the pilot that I will help investigate. Since I'm just a kid, the hijacker might let his guard down and give him or herself away. The pilot tells me to return to my seat, and to remain calm.

Slowly I make my way down the aisle of the plane glancing at each passenger. By the time I get to the back of the plane, I have narrowed my suspicions to two people. The most obvious is the woman sitting next to me. She is wearing _____ _____ and carrying _____ _____ . When I look at her, she _____ _____ .

The other is a man a few rows back who is writing with a thick, dark pen. He is wearing _____ . Sticking out of his pocket is _____ . When he catches me looking at him, he _____ _____ .

I return to the front of the plane and quickly turn around to see if anyone is watching me. _____ seems to be looking my way. It could be just a coincidence. While I pretend to wait for the restroom to become vacant, I whisper to the pilot, "I think I know who it is." At that moment the flight attendant shoves me into the restroom and closes the door. Is she involved too? I pull my ticket envelope out of my pocket and scribble a note to the pilot. It says, "_____ _____ _____ ."

The pilot announces to the passengers to prepare for an emergency landing. He begins his descent…

On another sheet of paper, write the story's ending.

Kick Flips and Ollies

AJ brought his new skateboard to the school parking lot on Saturday morning where all the skaterboarders gather to practice their tricks. He decided to watch and listen to see what he could learn.

"Did you see that kick flip? He must have gotten 3 feet of air, and he still came right down on his board after it spun around!"

"I've been working on a 180 kick flip, but I can only get my board to turn 1/4 of the way."

"I'd be happy if I could do an ollie, but I still can't get off the ground."

"Try stepping back on the tail like you're popping a wheelie. Then flick the nose down with your front foot so the board is level under both feet. That's it!"

AJ watched in amazement as the skaters seemed to fly through the air on their boards, sometimes spinning the board in midair before landing on it again. Sometimes they even turned so they were facing the opposite direction from which they started. "Kick flips and ollies! Those tricks are too advanced for me," thought AJ. "I think I'll go watch the guys over by the curb. They look like they're doing easier tricks."

"Who can do a nose slide all the way across the curb?"

AJ watched as the guys seemed to slide the front of their skateboards along the curb.

"Tail slides back the other way!"

Now they were going back along the curb sliding on the back end of the skateboard. "It looks like you have to figure out how to get the right end of your board up on the curb first," reasoned AJ as he saw two skaters tick-tacking toward him.

"Hey, Dude! You're new here, aren't you? We only started last week. Come on with us," invited the boys.

AJ imitated them as they leaned back on the tail and lifted the front wheels and pivoted on the rear wheels.

Then they did the same thing leaning on the nose, lifting the back wheels and pivoting on the front wheels. Continuing this motion they were able to make their way across the parking lot.

That night AJ dreamed he was able to do an ollie over a fire hydrant. With enough practice, his dream may come true.

Unless you are a skateboarder, you probably found several new terms or vocabulary words. But the story provided context clues.

Choose the correct answer by circling, filling in the blank, numbering, etc.

1. A skater is someone who: a) rides a skateboard,   b) roller skates,   c) ice skates.

2. Number these tricks from easiest to most difficult:

    ___ nose slide   ___ kick flip   ___ tick-tack

3. In which trick does the board spin around in the air?_____

4. Describe an ollie._____

    _____

    _____

Land of Dinosaurs

Can you imagine what life would be like if humans and dinosaurs were alive at the same time? That's what author and illustrator James Gurney imagined when he wrote *Dinotopia*. In this story, Professor Denison and his son Will set out on a voyage. When a typhoon hit, they were shipwrecked and tossed into the raging sea. A school of dolphins came to their rescue and brought them to an unusual island where dinosaurs and humans lived together peacefully. In fact, they helped each other.

Dinotopia is the journal of the Denisons' adventures on this island. With a Protoceratops as their guide, the father and son visit a hatchery where people help with the birth and raising of young dinosaurs. They journey to a town built on top of a volcano, and another built in the middle of a waterfall.

The only way into the city is on a flying vessel which looks very much like a Pterosaur. Riding an Apatosaurus as if it were a horse, they encounter a Tyrannosaurus Rex, a not so friendly dinosaur, even in *Dinotopia*. In another village they live in tree houses and learn to do tricks such as sky hopping from the neck of a Brachiosaurus. As they spend time with the dinosaurs, they learn to communicate in their language, which is very musical. Not only is it a fascinating adventure, but the pictures in the book capture one's imagination.

At one point Will and his dad are separated when his dad explores a mysterious hidden canyon, and Will flies

off on a Skybax. Where do they end up? Will they see each other again? Do Will and his dad ever return to civilization as we know it? Read *Dinotopia* to find the answers.

Complete each statement by circling the correct answer.

1. James Gurney's purpose in writing *Dinotopia* was ...
   a. to explain how life once was on Earth.
   b. to show how humans and dinosaurs could live peacefully together.
   c. to show how impossible it would be for humans and dinosaurs to live together.

2. One way dinosaurs helped people in *Dinotopia* was by ...
   a. providing transportation for people.
   b. doing all the work.
   c. fighting all the enemies.

3. One way people helped the dinosaurs in the story was by ...
   a. fighting the dinosaurs' enemies.
   b. painting pictures of them.
   c. helping with the birth and raising of the young.

4. The purpose of the article on *Dinotopia* was ...
   a. to teach me about dinosaurs.
   b. to interest me in reading the book for myself.
   c. to answer the question of whether or not it is possible for dinosaurs and humans to live together peacefully.

Thinking Cap: Do you think a civilization like Dinotopia could be possible? Why or why not?_____

_____

What's Gnu at the Zoo?

"There is a problem at the zoo," explained Mr. Limb as the class rode down the road on the bus. All the animals are getting sick and no one can figure out why. Our class has been selected to help solve the mystery. When we arrive, each pair of students will be assigned to an animal. Take a pear with you for a snack. We'll meet back near the kitchen at 12:00 for lunch.

Ryan and Wes went to the lion's cage and found him lying on the ground, tied to a stake. While they watched, the zookeeper tossed him some food. He ate eight steaks and then lay down again.

Wade and Billy were assigned to the bear's cage. When they arrived, it looked bare because the bear was hiding in its cave.

Stacy and Lataya arrived at the deer enclosure just in time to see them feeding. "Oh dear!" exclaimed Stacy. That doe just ate a whole lump of dough. Now she's lying down in that hole."

As Nick and Latisha walked to the eagle's perch, Nick asked, "Is it legal to keep an ill eagle?"

To see the buffalo, Jill and Elise flew in a small plane over the plains at the edge of the zoo. "I wonder if buffalo catch a cold or flu like people do?" remarked Jill.

At the farm area of the zoo, Morgan said to Kristy, "Oh, you can tell that poor ewe isn't feeling well. What is it she's eating?"

As Tyler and Michael made their way to the elephant section, Tyler commented, "I heard that herd of elephants bellowing as we arrived. They sounded miserable!"

The fourth-grade class met

near the kitchen at noon to have lunch and discuss their experiences. "What is that horrible smell?" asked Wes. It was coming from the kitchen. The cook who prepared the food for the animals knew she had been caught and admitted to making the animals sick.

"What a tale we have to tell when we return to school!"

Homophones are two or more words that sound the same but are spelled differently and have different meanings.

Read through the story again and circle the homophones. Connect each pair with a line. Example: We rode down the road.

Fill in the missing homophone for each of the following.

night: _____   some: _____   sun:_____

two: _____   which: _____   none: _____

Here are more sets of homophones. Write a sentence for each pair.

1. hare – hair: _____

_____

2. mane – main: _____

_____

3. sail – sale: _____

_____

4. male – mail: _____

_____

Snowballs in Space

A **dictionary** gives a definition for a word. It also tells you how to pronounce the word and what part of speech it is, such as a noun or a verb.

An **encyclopedia** gives you a more detailed description of your word or topic. It might tell you about the history of it, give you scientific information about it, or give specific examples.

A **newspaper** or magazine will tell you about what is currently happening or has just recently happened. Here are examples from each of these three sources telling about the same topic: comets.

Dictionary

comet: (kŏm´ ĭt) n. A heavenly body moving around the sun in an off-center orbit. It contains a bright head and usually a tail that streams away from the sun.

Newspaper

March 17, 1997. The Hale-Bop Comet is making a grand appearance in the northeastern sky just before sunrise. Those who are not early risers can wait a few days until after March 20. From then through the month of April it will be visible low in the northwest sky just after dusk. The best time to view the comet will be between March 26 and April 12 because there will be no moonlight to block out the light of the comet.

Encyclopedia

Comet. A comet resembles a fuzzy star and travels along a definite path through the solar system. The center is called the nucleus. It is about 10 miles in diameter. It is surrounded by a hazy cloud called a *coma*. The diameter of the coma may be almost a million miles. It may also form a tail that can extend as far as 100 million miles.

Scientists believe the nucleus is like a dirty snowball made up of dust particles and ices of various kinds. As it approaches the sun, heat causes the outer layers to vaporize. Dust and gases are released to form the coma. The smallest particles are pushed away and form the tail.

A

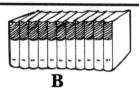

B

C

Write the letter of the resource you would use to . . .

_____ find a definition of a comet.

_____ find out current information about a comet.

_____ find out what a comet is made of.

_____ find out when you can see a specific comet in the sky.

_____ find out about the specific parts of a comet.

_____ find out the correct pronounciation of the word.

Answer the following.

1. What is a comet?_____

_____

2. Name the three parts of a comet._____

_____

3. What is the name of the comet that was visible in March and April of 1997? _____

Five-Minute Conversation

"Hi Sarah. My mom will allow me to talk for only five minutes. Can you believe it?"asked Hannah.

"My mom threatens to do the same," replied Sarah. "What's up?"

"Two things," responded Hannah. "First, what's the math assignment? I forgot to write it down."

"Page 279. You only have to do the odds. It's pretty easy. What's the second thing? I hope it's more exciting than the first."

"It is. Remember the house across the street that's been for sale? Well, there was a moving van there when I came home from school," remarked Hannah.

"So, who's moving in? Anybody fun?" questioned Sarah.

"Wait till you hear this! There's a girl who looks like she's about our age, so I walked over and asked if I could help them. You'll never guess what she was carrying!" exclaimed Hannah.

"Well, tell me quickly before your time is up!"

"Okay. It was a saddle. She has her very own horse! Can you believe it? I told her I always dreamed of having a horse, and she said I could ride it sometime." Hannah poured out excitedly.

"She'll probably be your new best friend," Sarah said with a lump in her throat.

"Don't be silly, Sarah. You'll always be my best friend. Why don't you come over and meet her too?"

" I'll be there in a minute."

"Okay. See ya!"

"Bye!"

When you write, you must use quotations marks whenever you are recording someone's words. Notice that quotation marks are placed around only whatever a person actually said.

Add quotation marks to the sentences below. Be sure to include any punctuation mark inside the quotation marks.

1. What are you doing after school today? asked Hannah.

2. I don't know, replied Sarah. Do you have any good ideas?

3. Hannah responded, I thought we could invite the new girl, Ashley, over and show her our doll collection.

Use quotation marks and write a short conversation between you and a friend.

_____

_____

_____

_____

Extension: You could write a play for you and your friends to perform. Be sure to put each speaker's part in quotation marks.

The Sinking Behemoth

Belfast, Ireland, was the birthplace of the largest moving object built by human hands in 1912. Its name was the *Titanic*, the largest ship ever to sail the seas. She was 850 feet long and 90 feet wide. The distance from the keel to the deck was equal in height to a 10-story building. She was not only big, she was grand. Inside the massive boat were great staircases, stained-glass windows, beautiful chandeliers, libraries, a gymnasium, and a swimming pool. It took 3 years and hundreds of thousands of pounds of steel to build her. When launched, she looked invincible—the safest ship afloat.

On the tenth of April, 1912, the mighty *Titanic* sailed out of England bound for New York City holding 2,200 passengers. For four days she sailed on calm seas under a clear sky. But on the fifth day, disaster struck about 500 miles off the coast of Newfoundland. Traveling at a speed of 20.5 knots, the *Titanic* crashed into an iceberg which towered 50 feet above the water. The impact broke the ship's hull, and she rapidly began taking on water. Lifeboats were filled with women and children first, then quickly lowered. Because there were not enough lifeboats for everyone, more than 1,500 people died in the cold sea as the ship sank within $2^1/_2$ hours.

Eighty years later, survivors remember that night as clearly as if it were yesterday. One woman remembers her father standing on the sinking deck of the *Titanic* as she and her mother were lowered into a lifeboat. He was a great swimmer and told them not to worry about him. That was the last time they ever saw him.

Match the letter of each of the numbers on the right to the corresponding word or phrase on the left.

_____ years to build the *Titanic*   A. 1912

_____ miles from Newfoundland   B. 850

_____ people who died   C. 90

_____ height of the *Titanic*   D. 10
(number of stories)
                                                         E. 3
_____ length of the *Titanic*
                                                         F. hundreds of
_____ pounds of steel   thousands

_____ number of days on calm seas   G. 2,200

_____ height of iceberg   H. 4

_____ *Titanic* began maiden voyage   I. 5

_____ time it took the *Titanic* to sink   J. 500

_____ disaster struck on this day   K. 20.5

_____ width of the *Titanic*   L. 50

_____ speed the *Titanic* was traveling   M. 1,500

_____ number of passengers on board   N. $2^1/_2$

Extension: Find out more about this famous ship. Robert Ballard has written a fascinating book about his attempt to explore the remains of the *Titanic* at the bottom of the ocean.

Last-Minute Stardom

It was time for the play to begin and the lead actress had not arrived. When the door opened, everyone looked up expecting to see Beth.

"I hate to put a damper on things, but Beth has a fever and cannot possibly make it tonight," explained her mom.

"Well, I never put all my eggs in one basket," responded Ms. King. "Amanda has been our understudy for that part and knows it well. Amanda, put on Beth's costume."

Amanda was on cloud nine as she jumped off the stage after the performance and ran to where her family and friends were waiting at the back of the auditorium.

"You were terrific, Honey. You stole the show!" exclaimed Dad.

"You always were the apple of my eye," added Grandma.

"You only see a performance done that well once in a blue moon," added Grandpa.

"How time flies. It seems like just yesterday you were just a baby in my arms and now you're the star of your school play," cried Mom as she gave Amanda a hug.

Amanda was speechless as everyone complimented her.

"What's the matter, has the cat got your tongue?" asked her big brother.

"Speaking of cats," said Dad, "it's raining cats and dogs outside. Grandpa, you keep an eye on everyone while I run and get the car."

As they waited, Ms. King walked by. "I thought we were walking on thin ice when we learned Beth couldn't be here.

But you were fantastic, Amanda. There's no end to what you can do, even when you're down to the wire."

It seemed like an eternity before Dad returned. "Sorry it took so long. The traffic is slower than molasses in January. I avoided an accident in the parking lot only by the skin of my teeth."

"I get shotgun!" shouted Amanda's brother as they ran out to the car.

An idiom is an expression that means something different from what it actually says. Each picture illustrates an idiom in the story. Under the picture write what each idiom really means.

  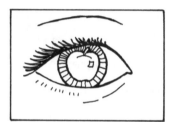

_____   _____   _____

_____   _____   _____

Draw a simple picture for the idioms below taken from the story.

 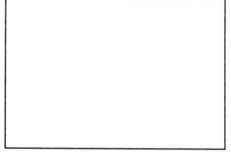

Everyone liked your part best.

It's raining really hard.

Toys of Old

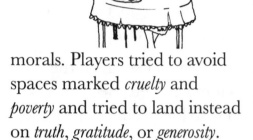

The 1990s is a great time to be a kid. More toys and games are available than ever.

Back in the 1800s children didn't have as much leisure time as children today. They were expected to do many more chores around the house and farm. As some families moved to cities and gained wealth, toys were given to their children. But even their play had purpose: to develop morals as well as physical and social skills. Dolls came with trunks full of clothes of the latest fashions. By dressing the dolls, girls learned the proper way to dress. A game called *grace hoops* used sticks and a ring that players tossed back and forth without letting the ring touch their hands. In playing this game, girls were supposed to learn to move with grace. The first board game manufactured in America was intended to teach morals. Players tried to avoid spaces marked *cruelty* and *poverty* and tried to land instead on *truth*, *gratitude*, or *generosity*.

During the early 1900s miniature models of adult tools and machines were favorite toys. Girls had stoves, washing machines, and brooms, while boys played with toy hammers and screw drivers. In 1903, Teddy Bears, named for President Teddy Roosevelt who refused to kill a bear while hunting, became a popular stuffed animal. Pink Silly Putty, invented in 1943, was fun to bounce and stretch.

Today, games and toys have a different focus. Many of them are meant to educate. Some games encourage kids to learn more about the world or stimulate creativity. But others are purely for entertainment.

Children today also have the advantage of technology, so interactive computer and video games are popular.

What will the toys of the future be like? Which toys will remain popular? What new toys will take their place?

Compare toys of the past, present, and future. Where the circles overlap, write the things they have in common. In the outer portions, write the things that are unique to each time period. In the circle labeled "Future," write what you think toys of the future will have in common or how they will differ from other time periods.

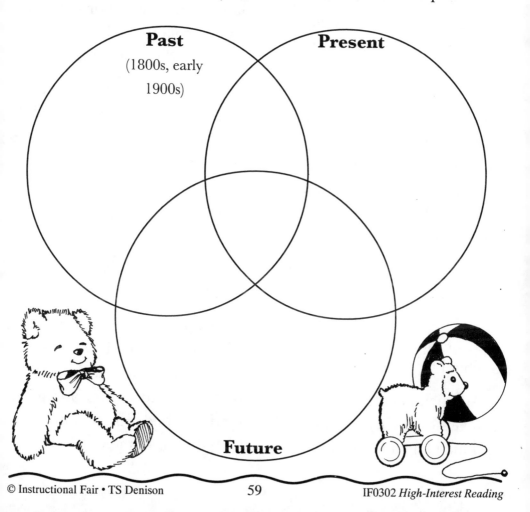

Past
(1800s, early 1900s)

Present

Future

A Day in the Lives of...

Kristy and Nicole were best friends. They had lived next door to each other all their lives. But as they were getting older, they began to drift apart from one another. Let's follow them for a day and see if we can find out why.

Kristy woke up at 7:00 A.M. and got dressed for school. She sat down with her family and ate a grapefruit, toast and egg, and a glass of milk for breakfast. She brushed her teeth, grabbed her book bag and bike helmet, and rode off to school. She had quit stopping for Nicole because she was never ready on time.

Nicole rolled out of bed at 7:45, threw on her clothes, and grabbed a Pop Tart to eat in the car as her mom drove her to school.

At lunch Nicole and Kristy sat together. Kristy emptied her lunch bag and began eating her tuna sandwich, apple, and yogurt. Nicole began munching on her chips, baloney sandwich and chocolate pudding while drinking a can of cola to wash it down. Kristy had milk with her lunch.

After school, Kristy went straight to soccer practice while Nicole went home and watched television.

For dinner that night, Kristy's family ate tacos with rice and beans, lettuce, tomatoes, and cheese. Nicole's family had hot dogs and french fries.

After dinner the two girls got together to do their homework. When they finished, Kristy went home to shower and get ready for bed. She was in bed by 9:00 P.M. so she would be

well-rested for school tomorrow. Nicole played video
games until 10:30 and then got
ready for bed.

Let's compare the lifestyles of these two girls, Kristy and Nicole.
Fill in the chart below with specific examples from the story.

	Kristy	**Nicole**
Foods eaten during the day.		
Exercise		
Care of body		

We live in a throw-away society. When something is worn out, we
throw it away and get something new. Some people think we can
treat our bodies that way. But the body we have now is the only
one we get so we must take proper care of it. Which of these girls
will probably have a healthier body? _____

Why? _____

_____

Tell why you think these best friends are drifting apart from one
another.

_____

_____

Where Did Ramona Come From?

Some people like to write books that take readers away to fantasy worlds, where anything is possible. Not Beverly Cleary. When Beverly was in the third grade, she thought school books were boring. But when she discovered the library, she learned to love reading. Although she enjoyed fairy tales, Beverly would rather read about normal, everyday people living in a typical neighborhood. That's when she decided she would write those kinds of books when she grew up.

Her own hometown of Portland, Oregon, became the setting for her stories about Ramona Quimby and Henry Huggins. They are kids who clank around on coffee cans and string stilts just as Beverly Cleary did as a young girl. The characters share other experiences with Beverly also. She was teased for naming a doll Fordson Lafayette after a neighbor's tractor. In another of her books, Ramona is teased for naming her doll Chevrolet, after her aunt's car.

Beverly has a great imagination. Once she found some flowers called bachelor's buttons and sewed them on her father's jacket in place of missing buttons. The characters in her books share that quality by being very creative people.

Good observation skills also helped Beverly become a good author. It's the little details that really could happen that make her stories realistic.

Answer the following questions about Beverly Cleary.

1. Beverly Cleary has written more than 30 books for children. Based on the article, "Where Did Ramona Come From?" where did Cleary get her ideas for her stories?

   _____

2. What are three qualities that make Beverly Cleary a good author?

   _____

   _____

   _____

3. What is one of Beverly Cleary's favorite pastimes?

   _____

Thinking Cap: Think about your own life and the things that interest you. Make a list of experiences that you think could be turned into a series of fun and exciting short stories.

Extension: Read one of Beverly Cleary's books. *Henry Huggins* and *Ramona Quimby, Age 8,* are two of them.

La Fiesta

Come for a ride with me just outside of *Santa Fe*. We'll drive through the colorful red rock *canyons* and up onto the *mesa* where the *vista* of the surrounding countryside is spectacular. This is the land of cowboys. If you look down into the valley, you might see a *rodeo* with cowboys riding bucking *broncos* and throwing their *lassos* to rope a bull's horns. There is a grand house up on this mesa which belongs to the Martinez family. Today is the tenth birthday of their daughter Maria, and everyone is invited to her party. The guests gather on the *patio* where tables are laden with *tacos*, *tortilla* chips and *salsa*, *bananas*, *mangos*, and two birthday cakes, one *chocolate* and one *vanilla*. To entertain the guests, a group of musicians are playing *guitars* and *tambourines*.

The best part of the party is the breaking of the *piñata* that hangs from a tree next to the patio. Maria is blindfolded first and handed a stick which she swings at the *piñata* while her papa keeps it moving from side to side and up and down. Smack! Maria hits it. Now it is another child's turn.

After each one tries, the *piñata* finally breaks open. The children rush in as candy and prizes shower down. They gather as much as they can hold and hurry to give their treasures to their mamas to hold while they rush back for more. As the sun sets over the *mesa*, the air becomes cool, and people put on their *ponchos* for warmth. When the *mosquitoes* come out for their feast, it is time for us to go home.

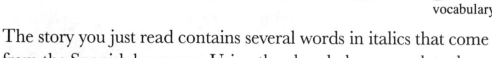

The story you just read contains several words in italics that come from the Spanish language. Using the clues below, complete the crossword puzzle with the correct Spanish words from the story.

Across

4. a view
5. a fruit
7. sweet treat made from cocoa
9. event where cowboys display their skills
10. outside porch or paved courtyard
13. deep cut between mountains
15. an insect
16. sauce made with tomatoes
17. Mexican bread made from corn or wheat flour

Down

1. an untamed horse
2. a rhythm instrument
3. city in New Mexico
4. a flavor
6. a cowboy's rope
8. outer covering, like a blanket with a head hole
11. a food: meat and cheese in a crispy shell
12. a decorated papier-mâché object stuffed with candy and treats
14. a string instrument
15. a flat-topped hill

Summer Storm

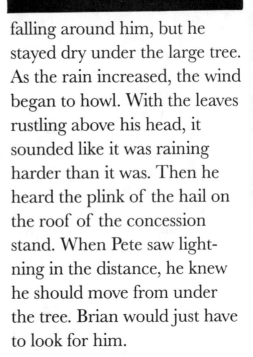

Brian went zooming to the park on his bike. He was meeting his buddies for an afternoon of hoops. It started out as a perfect day, until Brian's Mom made him drag his little brother Pete along.

"Wait for me, Brian," whined Pete as he tried to keep up. It was almost as annoying as a buzzing mosquito.

Brian parked his bike and followed his nose to the concession stand. There were burgers sizzling on the grill, popcorn popping, and big barrels of fizzing root beer. He bought two burgers and two root beers. Then he walked Pete over to a nearby tree. Brian handed him his lunch and said, "Sit here and eat and don't move until I come back to get you." Brian ran off to meet his buddies.

As Pete began eating, he heard the pitter-patter of rain falling around him, but he stayed dry under the large tree. As the rain increased, the wind began to howl. With the leaves rustling above his head, it sounded like it was raining harder than it was. Then he heard the plink of the hail on the roof of the concession stand. When Pete saw lightning in the distance, he knew he should move from under the tree. Brian would just have to look for him.

Pete started running for shelter. Suddenly, the whole sky lit up as a splat of lightning and a boom of thunder hit at the same time. Looking behind him, Pete heard a loud moan and saw the top of the tree come crashing down right where he had been sitting. Brian saw it too, from the other side of the park.

"Pete!" he screamed as he ran, ignoring the pain of the hail pounding on his head. At the moment the lightning struck, Brian realized Pete was not the drag he thought he was.

Brian thought he heard his name as he ran, but then wondered if it was the wind playing tricks on him. There it was again. "Brian!" That voice had never sounded so good.

This story is full of words whose sounds make you think of what they mean, such as "buzzing" and "fizzing." Use the clues to find words like these in the story. The letters in the boxes will spell the name of this type of word.

1. moving rapidly

2. sharp, metallic sound

3. loud wailing cry

4. deep sound like a cannon

5. to bang noisily

6. soft, crackling sound

7. a short, quick sound

8. a series of light, quick tapping sounds

9. a long, thin cry

10. a hissing noise

11. a load, smacking sound

Squeezing Water from the Sky

Chungungo, a little desert village in Chile between the coast and El Tofo Mountain, had no water. There were no rivers or lakes and it never rained. Even though clouds and fog passed over the village regularly they left no moisture behind. The clouds would go over the mountain but would then evaporate over the desert.

On a mountain nearby there was a grove of eucalyptus trees which were always wet, almost as if it were raining just on the grove of trees. Scientists studied the trees to find out how they were able to capture water. They discovered that when the low clouds, or fog, rolled over the mountain, tiny droplets of water stuck on the leaves. The droplets ran together to form bigger drops which fell to the ground. So the trees and ground there were always wet.

The scientists experimented with this idea of getting water drops from fog until they developed a plan to help the people of Chungungo. This was their plan. They would set large plastic nets upright on the mountain like sails on a boat. When the fog rolled over the mountain, droplets would stick to the plastic like they did to the leaves. The droplets would then run down to the ground where they would be collected and piped down the mountain to the people in the village.

It worked! The people of Chungungo now had water in the village. Where there once were no trees or plants, there were now beautiful gardens.

1. Draw a diagram showing how water got from the mountaintop to the village below.

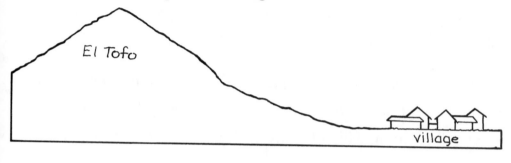

2. How did the grove of eucalyptus trees help the scientists to think of this plan?

_____

_____

3. What effect will this have on the village?

_____

_____

4. What would be necessary in order for scientists to use this same idea to bring water to other desert areas?

_____

_____

5. Will another area be too dry because of the way this water was taken for Chungungo? Why or why not?

_____

_____

Thinking Cap: Can you think of another way of bringing water to dry areas?

The Case of the Missing Lemonheads

Below is a mystery story that you will help write. Read the whole story first. Then go back and fill in the blanks. You get to determine the guilty person and explain why. Be creative!

My dad always told me I was good at solving mysteries, so I decided to set up my own private eye business. My headquarters was my bedroom, which I share with my trusted canine assistant, a Jack Russell Terrier named Puddles. She has a great nose for sniffing things out, so I figured she might come in handy on some cases. My first client was my cousin Joel, who was visiting for the summer. He moved in with our family which consists of my dad and mom, my three sisters, and me, Larry. Joel's mom had sent him a box of treats, including his favorite candy, lemonheads. The problem was that Joel's lemonheads were disappearing faster than he was eating them. So he asked if I could help him find the thief.

I needed some background information. I asked Joel where he kept his lemonheads. He was reluctant to tell me at first, but I finally coaxed it out of him. I think he was afraid that if I knew where they were, I might dip into his stash. He finally told me he kept them _____ .

Next, I needed to know if anyone suspicious had entered Joel's room. Seems that two days ago my oldest sister Amanda, who is 14, was wearing Joel's one-of-a-kind _____ sweatshirt. So it's possible she might have gone into his room to get it. Melissa, my 12-year-old sister, was seen going in there yesterday to get Puddles who had wandered into Joel's room. My youngest sister, Rebecca, also ventured in yesterday to borrow a CD. Mom had to go in to collect the laundry, and Dad went in to change a light bulb. Every member of the family had been in Joel's room, so everyone was a possible suspect.

Now it was necessary to look for clues. I figured the most obvious clues would be lemonhead wrappers, lemon breath, a yellow tongue, and sticky fingers. So I began my investigation.

Rebecca was sitting at the piano. I went in to watch her play when I noticed _____

_____ .

Hmm, I thought. Could be. Now I had to check the others.

In the meantime I gave Puddles a lemonhead wrapper to sniff and commanded her to sniff out more. She picked up the wrapper in her teeth and _____

_____ .

I offered to help Mom with the laundry so I could check everyone's pockets. Mom was surprised I offered to help and asked if I was sick. That's when I smelled her lemon breath. Hmm. A possibility, but not likely. After all, she's always warning us about how bad candy is for our teeth. She also drinks lemon-flavored tea. But I had to keep all my options open. As I began

checking pockets I found _____
_____ .

A few minutes later Melissa came into the kitchen to get a snack. I
discovered _____ ____
_____ .

    Amanda was the hardest. She's always off playing with her
friends. But today was my lucky day. She came home because her
friends had to visit their grandmother. I hid under her bed and
found that _____
_____ .

    Now I had all the evidence I needed. I was certain that it must
be _____ because _____
_____ .

I just had to get _____ to admit to it. So, I set a trap.
I _____
_____ .

    To my surprise _____ fell for the trap and it
turned out _____ had been the guilty one all along.
Joel found a new hiding place for his lemonheads and he gave me
three of them for solving the mystery.

Extension: For more fun mysteries, read other Encyclopedia
              Brown books.